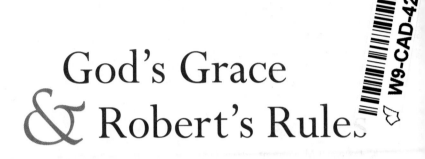

God's Grace
& Robert's Rules

A Theological Primer for Vestry Members

Richard Kunz

ISBN 978-0-88028-412-7

Printed in USA

God's Grace
& Robert's Rules

A Theological Primer for Vestry Members

Richard Kunz

Forward Movement
Cincinnati, Ohio

This guide is dedicated to my father, the Rev. W. Richard Kunz, who taught me theology through his life, and to the Rt. Rev. Robert Appleyard, the Rev. William Mills, and the Very Rev. George Werner, who started me on my course.

Table of Contents

1. DIVINE AND HUMAN   3
The Two Natures of the Church

Since Jesus was both human and divine, his body,
the Church, will also have two natures. It is a human
institution, but it is also a spiritual reality. Having a healthy
church means growing fully into both of those natures.

2. FAITH AND ACTION   9
Challenge and Opportunity

Faith involves perceiving what God is calling us to do.
In order for a church to act in faith, the members of the
vestry must discern God's will together.

Preface

I have been blessed with a long and varied vocation as a priest in The Episcopal Church. I have served on the staff of a cathedral, as vicar of an inner-city mission, rector of a suburban parish, executive director of a mission in Honduras, and currently as rector of an urban parish. I have experienced exciting, creative ministry and times of conflict and challenge. I have had the privilege of seeing God at work through the church in all those situations and have tried to learn from both the successes and failures.

When I graduated from seminary, my head was full of ideas about preaching, theology, pastoral care, and mission. What I had not prepared for was the everyday running of a congregation. I was guilty of viewing vestries, with their focus on budgets, roof leaks, signage, maintenance, and other nitty-gritty items, as disconnected from the real issues of ministry.

I have come to see that service on the vestry is a rich and wonderful avenue for ministry and spiritual growth. Lots of people have ideas about what the church "should" do. Vestry members are the ones tasked with turning theory into practice. They take stock of the resources of the congregation and discern the best match between gifts and needs. They make the church's mission possible.

The vestry also sets the tone for the rest of the congregation. Bitterness and division among vestry members almost always spills over into the rest of the congregation. A vestry that thinks only of preserving the status quo will hold the parish back from creative outreach and ministry. A vestry willing to prayerfully do the work of spiritual discernment and to support one another in decisions will be a unifying force for healthy growth and ministry.

There are many rich sources of guidance and enrichment for vestry members. Forward Movement, the publisher of this guide, offers several resources, including *The Restoration Project* and *Good News: A Scriptural Path to Reconciliation*. Episcopal Church Foundation is committed to providing tools to develop and strengthen leaders, especially their Vital Practices and Vital Teams programs. The *Vestry Resource Guide*, developed by ECF and published by Forward Movement, provides a systematic introduction to the role of vestries, with loads of practical advice and teachings. *God's Grace and Robert's Rules* offers a different focus, encouraging vestries to connect practical issues with our ideas about God. I also hope to give vestry members a way to see their service in church leadership as a means of personal spiritual growth, not just as an obligation or task.

Different congregations use different terminology: parish or mission; rector, priest-in-charge, or vicar; vestry or mission council, etc. For ease of language, this book primarily uses rector and parish, but the principles apply regardless of the terminology or the size of the congregation.

I hope this primer will enrich your own vestry involvement and help you live more fully into God's call for your life and for your congregation.

Richard Kunz

Introduction

The opportunity to serve on a vestry is a privilege. It is also usually a growth experience. Sometimes that growth is pleasant and exhilarating. Sometimes it comes with pain and frustration. In both cases, the growth comes from close engagement with the issues that make our congregations "church." A church is a unique creature, and the characteristics that make it distinctive

> **Although it sounds complicated, theology is simply our way of speaking about God.**

have their roots in theology. Although it sounds complicated, theology is simply our way of speaking about God. Who do we think God is? How does God relate to humanity? What are we hoping for when we attend worship? What is it that Christians have learned about God from centuries of trying to follow Jesus? If the church is truly called together by God, then it will reflect God's nature.

Imagine a board grappling with a new initiative. One member, an accomplished and intelligent business person, believes the idea is a financial disaster, well beyond the management capacity of the church staff and volunteers. Another member, just as intelligent and accomplished, agrees that it looks unlikely but argues that the board simply needs to have faith, and God will provide the resources needed.

Both of these earnest leaders are acting from their understanding of Church. They are both eager for their congregation to be healthy and to act in accordance with God's will. But they are probably both caught up in incomplete theologies and spiritualities that keep them from reaching a creative solution. Unfortunately, this kind of conflict often leads to people being regarded as either caring only about the bottom line or being lost in the clouds. In fact, their conflict is built into the nature of "Church" and cannot be resolved without looking at it in theological context. Christian theology teaches us that there are some things that always need to be held in tension: Jesus was divine and human, we are saints and sinners, our life is earthly and heavenly, we are both individuals and part of an interconnected whole. As we deal with the practical realities of church life, we will find ourselves trying to find the proper balance between those tensions.

Robert's Rules offers guidelines on decorum and on ways to make meetings more efficient and productive. A good organizational structure is an important component of an effective vestry. But the purpose of this book is to offer theological and spiritual context on various issues that confront church leaders. Theology is not just an academic discipline. Spirituality is not inherently impractical. Our creeds and the scriptures grow out of the living experience of the church, and the nature of the church reflects these insights and realities.

This book is written for those who serve on church vestries. My hope is that they will benefit from it in two ways. First, vestry members will gain a deeper understanding of Christian theology as they apply it to concrete situations. Secondly, they will have a much more satisfying experience of serving together and will be better equipped to face the challenges God puts before them during their time of service.

CHAPTER ONE

Divine and Human:
The Two Natures of the Church

For the right Faith is, that we believe and confess, that our Lord Jesus Christ, the Son of God, is God and Man; Perfect God and Perfect Man; Who although he be God and Man, yet he is not two, but one Christ. (from the Creed of Saint Athanasius)

In the beginning was the Word, and the Word was with God, and the Word was God. And the Word became flesh and lived among us, and we have seen his glory, the glory as of a father's only son, full of grace and truth. (John 1:1,14)

Now you are the body of Christ and individually members of it. (1 Corinthians 12:27)

One of the first major theological challenges faced by the early church was trying to come to terms with the nature of Jesus. Who was he, and in what way did he represent God? What did it mean to say he was Lord? Some passages in the New Testament, as in the first chapter of John's Gospel, indicate that Christ existed before creation and is divine. Other passages emphasize the humanity of Christ and can be interpreted to mean that Jesus was like any other human being, filled with God's Spirit in the same way as the prophets.

These two scriptural strands developed into opposing theologies. One side focused on the divinity of Christ. They argued that since Jesus was

God, he could not possibly have been human as well. How could God limit God's self to a single human existence? This thinking led these followers to believe that Jesus only appeared to be human, with the emphasis on appeared. His true nature was fully divine, and he did not share our human nature. Walking down the beach with his disciples, he left no footprints in the sand, as he had no true human body. He was able to look down at the crucifixion from a distance, as what was being crucified was an appearance, not the real Jesus.

Others focused on the humanity of Jesus. They believed that he was born like any other human, chosen by God for a particular mission. Led and empowered by God's Spirit, Jesus fulfilled that mission on behalf of humanity. But followers of this understanding didn't speak of incarnation. God and humanity remained separate categories. Jesus may have been godly, but, they believed, he was not God. If Jesus was simply one human among others, then his mission and ministry were not necessarily unique nor had God actually shared in our suffering or come to be among us.

Eventually in 451 CE at the Council of Chalcedon, after almost three hundred years of intense conflict that would make even the worst of vestry meetings look tame, the Church settled on a simple formula. Jesus was fully God but also fully human. Both sides held a portion of the truth—but only insofar as that portion was balanced in tension with the opposite truth. It is very important to note that the conclusion was not that Jesus was partly human and partly divine, some compromise between the two. If you read the Athanasian Creed, you will see painstaking efforts to make it clear that his divinity and his humanity both stand complete. Jesus is not "either/or" and is not "in between." He is "both."

This sounds like an obscure argument, but it is not. And this dual nature has direct relevance to vestries. If the church is now the Body of Christ, his continuing presence in the world, it makes sense that the church also has a dual nature. The church is a human institution. And it is a divine reality. Efforts to make it just one or the other will always result in heresy.

It follows that a certain amount of tension and conflict are built into the nature of the church. There are always two sides that need to be held in tension, or we lose our true nature.

This is why the "practical" board member and the "spiritual" board member need one another. They are not enemies. They both represent important theological realities.

> **The church is a human institution. And it is a divine reality. Efforts to make it just one or the other will always result in heresy.**

The church is a fully human institution, living in this world. That human, institutional reality is an essential part of its nature. God could have chosen to operate in a purely "spiritual" way, but instead, God chose to include human beings in salvation history. God chose to be present in the world through human beings bonded together in love by the good news of the life, death, and resurrection of Jesus.

So, instead of isolated individuals walking around having their own mystical experiences, we have a human community gathering for worship, teaching, ministry, and mission. And whenever two or more decide to get together, you have the beginnings of an organization. They need to decide when and where to meet. How long will the meeting last? What will they discuss? Will they sit on chairs? Meet outside? Will they want coffee? Because a church involves lots of people meeting regularly over time, these questions need answers. The vestry and clergy play an important role in addressing these questions and more, from logistics to facilities to finances.

These are not necessary evils but an expression of the humanity of Christ that is affirmed by the creeds. One teaching of the Incarnation is that God chose to be present in the world as a human being. The amazing good news of the Incarnation is that God shows us that human life can be a fit vehicle for God's full presence. Jesus, being human, had to take care of necessities like the ones above. He got hungry and cold, thirsty and tired. He could only be in one place at a time. He had to organize his life. If Jesus had ignored his health, become sickly or weak, or been wishy-washy in his organization, if he had failed to follow through on things he intended and promised, allowed his followers to distract him from his mission, fallen into the traps his enemies laid for him, or been delinquent in paying his bills, he would not have been faithful to the saving work God had called him to do. His presence in the world, and his identification with us in our humanity, was a precious part of his saving work.

Of course, Jesus did not spend his life just thinking about these things. He quotes scripture that says, "One does not live by bread alone, but by every word that comes from the mouth of God" (Matthew 4:4). He says, "But strive first for the kingdom of God and his righteousness, and all these things will be given to you as well" (Matthew 6:33). He calls us to be born from above by God's Spirit. He teaches us that we are God's children and that matters of love and justice are ultimately more important than things that pass away. Jesus devotes his energy to the mission and ministry given to him, and he demonstrates the generosity of God's love through healings, by delivering people from evil, and by teaching about the kingdom. These actions reflect Jesus' divinity. He is not content simply to be comfortable and take care of his own needs.

The church is a human organization. We are called to be as fully and healthily human as possible. We are called to institutional health. A church that is not properly cared for, behind in its bills, invisible to its community, or torn by destructive conflict is not a proper reflection of the full humanity of Christ.

But to simply be a healthy organization is not an end in itself. The church, like Christ, is also called to be divine. We are called to be full of God's Spirit. We are to share in the ministry of Christ in the world. We are meant to preach good news, to be a place where God can be experienced, and to value that which is unseen. We are called to live in faith.

As with Jesus, the tension between divine and human is not meant to be settled by a compromise. "Okay, our church will be a little less wealthy and materialistic, but also a little less spiritual." The church is meant to be healthy organizationally and also healthy spiritually. We are called to grow into the fullness that God has for us.

The doctrine of the Incarnation is that God has taken on human form. Jesus was fully human and fully divine. The church, as the Body of Christ, also has that dual reality. The decisions a vestry makes must honor both.

FOR PERSONAL REFLECTION

Do you most often think of Jesus as human or divine? How might your view affect the way you approach living as a Christian?

FOR GROUP DISCUSSION

Jesus is the only one who is perfect in his humanity and his divinity. When you look at your church, where do you see a healthy human institution? What are the signs of spiritual health?

In what areas is there room for growth or healing?

In your vestry meetings, is there a balance between institutional and spiritual? If not, in which direction does it tip?

CHAPTER TWO

Faith and Action:
Challenge and Opportunity

So faith by itself, if it has no works, is dead. (James 2:17)

By faith Abraham obeyed when he was called to set out for a place that he was to receive as an inheritance; and he set out, not knowing where he was going. (Hebrews 11:8)

If you indeed cry out for insight, and raise your voice for understanding; if you seek it like silver, and search for it as for hidden treasures—then you will understand the fear of the LORD and find the knowledge of God. Then you will understand righteousness and justice and equity, every good path. (Proverbs 2:3-5, 9)

To make decisions that honor both the full divinity and full humanity of Christ involves spiritual discernment. This can make vestry service a challenge for personal growth. Spiritual discernment is a process that leads to acting in faith.

Faith does not mean believing in the impossible, nor does it mean having convictions based on shaky evidence. I believe that faith is a kind of spiritual sight. God has revealed glimpses of the kingdom to us. God has given us ways to look forward and discern God's will. Faith is looking carefully at these glimpses and orienting our words and actions toward them. It is as if we see the faint gleam of a distant city on a far horizon and head toward that light, knowing it will lead us home, even if our vision is not perfect and there are distractions on the way.

So, for instance, it is clear that loving our neighbor is part of God's will. Depending on who the neighbor is, this dictate may be problematic. One of my former neighbors used to toss dead animals into our yard and had been known to shoot at some of the other neighbors with his BB gun. Choosing to love him seemed like an unlikely option, and, in fact, I failed at it. Looking back, I believe it would have been an act of faith to find ways to love him in spite of his behavior. The light of God's love was visible faintly on the horizon, but I chose a more adversarial path.

As individuals and churches, we are in a constant state of discernment. We generally know God's will for us. But our circumstances, challenges, and resources are constantly changing. So, the question becomes: "What does God want of us now in this particular situation?"

Sometimes the answer to that question is perfectly logical and obvious, and sometimes it takes more imagination. Discernment is the process of determining, to the best of our abilities, what actions will lead us closer to God's kingdom and help us to grow into the full humanity and divinity of Christ.

Often, people assume that faith will result in actions that seem bold and impractical, and good business sense will result in finding ways to act conservatively. I do not agree that this is the case. For example, the ideas of connecting the Atlantic and Pacific oceans by digging a massive canal, linking Staten Island and Brooklyn with a bridge, or building the Empire State Building, do not sound very conservative or logical. All these ideas seemed fantastical in their time. But they were, in fact, based on keen insights into what might be possible and profitable. To be visionary and to be businesslike should often go together.

There are times when faith calls us to humble service rather than flashy and grandiose actions. Faith may well call us to learn to live simply so that our resources can be used to feed the hungry or to have a balanced budget. Other times faith may call us to take bold risks that stretch us and seem at

As individuals and churches, we are in a constant state of discernment.

first impossible. What is important is to come, together, to our best understanding of what God is leading us to do, and then marshal our resources in the best way possible to act in obedience to that vision.

The end result should be something that is practical (even if it looks visionary at first) but also resonates with our beliefs and addresses our situations. It should be something that allows us to reflect both the healthy humanity and the redemptive divinity of Christ. To reach such a vision will involve discussion, prayer, research, more discussion, and courage. This is the process of discernment.

Many resources are available for learning about Christian discernment, especially from Ignatian and Quaker spiritualities. Concerned with discerning God's will, both the Jesuits and the Friends developed ways to make decisions that took careful account of inner motivations, scripture, the opinions of others, and moral and practical concerns. While most vestries likely will not delve deeply into those traditions, the underlying principles are important. In Christian discernment, many of the usual tools of decision-making are utilized, but hopefully the dynamic is different. In most groups, decision-making is reached by soliciting opinions from each individual and then working to get the rest of the group to agree. Eventually, one opinion prevails. The starting point for Christian discernment is the assumption that God is calling the group to something particular, and each person involved has some insight into what that might be. Rather than trying to pressure and manipulate others to a particular point of view, it is more productive for each member of the vestry to approach the issue with an attitude of openness to discovering together as a vestry what God has in mind. This involves listening to others, asking questions of them in order to understand their approach, and maintaining an attitude of respect for insights others might have. Even when some members hold out a strong objection to a decision most of the vestry has agreed upon, that objection may be very useful in anticipating some of the challenges involved in implementation.

Here's an example of this practice: A suburban church was approached by a growing private school that desired to use the Sunday school rooms during the week. The rooms were not being utilized except on Sunday mornings, but the Sunday school program was a dynamic one, and the church valued its children's activities highly. The potential rental income was very attractive and would open up new areas of ministry for the church. Most members of the vestry welcomed this new opportunity, but others were against it. They pictured the children showing up on Sunday mornings and being greeted, not by the Bible verses and art projects they had completed the week before, but by geometry charts and verb conjugations. They also pointed out that this arrangement would require extra hours for an already overworked sexton. The vestry consulted the Sunday school teachers and were able to address concerns. The school agreed to hire a cleaning service to prepare the rooms for Sunday morning. The result of the negotiations was a long and happy relationship between church and school that lasted for years.

Another critical element in Christian discernment is a willingness on the part of each member to fully support the decision made by the vestry. Everyone needs to be honest and to offer opinions during the discussion, but once a decision has been made, each member needs to commit to supporting it. Grumbling or other bad behavior undermine the vestry and its effectiveness. Sometimes the rest of the vestry will make a decision with which you disagree. Since the decision has come out of a discernment process, this is a time to put aside your individual opinion. Much better to say, "Our vestry has decided," than, "Those other vestry members made a bad decision." A willingness to function as a mature and united vestry will translate into a willingness to function as a mature and united congregation.

For faith to be a living thing that brings us together with God, it cannot be separated from the actions that flow from it. Our faith is lived out in the real world, not just in theory. A church is more than a building standing passively. A church is a living congregation that uses its building, along with its financial resources, leadership, and talents, to worship God, proclaim the gospel, and serve those in need. A vestry or church board is entrusted with managing the resources of a congregation. The vestry decides where those resources will be invested. In effect, the vestry puts the faith of a congregation into action.

FOR PERSONAL REFLECTION

What factors do I consider when making decisions in my own life? How are these decisions made? Does my faith enter into the process? Do I have an overall goal?

FOR GROUP DISCUSSION

What was a recent decision we felt good about? How did we reach that decision?

Do we regularly look toward the future in our decision-making? Do we have a process of corporate discernment?

Are we willing, once the vestry has reached a decision, to be united in support of that decision? How might that unity affect the parish? What behaviors might need to change to show this united spirit?

CHAPTER THREE

Sacraments: Outward and Visible Signs

Q. What are the sacraments?
A. The sacraments are outward and visible signs of inward and
spiritual grace, given by Christ as sure and certain means by which we
*receive that grace. (*The Book of Common Prayer, *p. 857)*

Philip said to him, "Lord, show us the Father, and we will be satisfied."
Jesus said to him, "Have I been with you all this time, Philip, and you
do not know me? Whoever has seen me has seen the Father...How can
you say, 'Show us the Father?'" (John 14:8-9)

Long ago God spoke to our ancestors in many and various ways by the
prophets, but in these last days he has spoken to us by a Son, whom he
appointed heir of all things, through whom he also created the worlds.
He is the reflection of God's glory and the exact imprint of God's very
being. (Hebrews 1:1-3a)

Sacramental theology flows from the theology of the Incarnation
and the dual nature of Christ. It is not just human beings who carry
God's life. Creation itself is meant to be an expression of God's love,
imparting life to God's creatures. Jesus can take bread and wine and
announce that he is present in them. As we learn in the Catechism
in *The Book of Common Prayer*, a sacrament is "an outward and visible
sign of inward and spiritual grace, given by Christ as sure and certain
means by which we receive that grace." In this definition we can see
the correlation with Jesus being both human and divine. We have the

visible signs, which are from creation, and also the divine grace, which they impart. If the Church, as the Body of Christ, is meant to be both human and divine, we can conclude that the church itself is a kind of sacrament. It has an outward and visible form, a sign of the spiritual grace given by Christ.

There are many implications to this, but let's focus on the church as building. In The Episcopal Church, one of the chief responsibilities of the vestry is to care for the church property. Even though the church canons (rules) dictate this obligation, getting vestry members to serve on the property committee can be a big challenge. Let's face it: making sure the toilets work and the light bulbs are energy efficient and the roof is sound does not have much of a leadership cachet. It sounds much better to be involved in outreach or evangelism or almost anything else! The mundane realities of keeping a building in good repair and functional do not seem very spiritual.

But I suggest that through the lens of Incarnation and sacramental theology, functional toilets and a leak-proof roof are just as spiritual as the outreach program. The church building and grounds are outward and visible signs of the spiritual grace present in the congregation.

In fact, most people who visit a church for the first time are acutely aware of the state of the building. I once visited a church with a floor so dirty that the legs of the kneeler crunched when it was lowered. Grit on the pews left a mark on my clothing. I did not return. The outward and visible sign of that church was that no one cared. They reluctantly went through the motions, with little thought or effort being put into their common life.

I have been to the opposite kind of a church as well. These churches reek of self-indulgence, their facilities screaming, "We have lots of money, and we are proud of our prosperity." This is not exactly the gospel message as I understand it. A church that insists on only the most expensive and stylish architecture or furnishings is probably calling the wrong kind of attention to itself and using its resources for things that do not point to God's kingdom.

Most churches seem to fall somewhere between those extremes. Many look as if they are enduring a kind of benign neglect. It is, perhaps, the same kind of neglect that your own family room may receive. People get comfortable, feel at home, and simply stop noticing the paint flaking off the front door or the musty smell in the meeting room. They would never return to a restaurant that had bathrooms in bad condition, but they don't think twice about the cracked toilet seats and slow drains in the bathrooms of the church basement. People look for schools that are bright and clean with well-equipped classrooms. But the same folks tend not to notice that the Sunday school rooms are damp and dimly lit, located in the "undercroft" (which sounds so much better than "basement"), with none of the equipment of a modern classroom. The building, in a sense, has become invisible to most of the members.

If the Church, as the Body of Christ, is meant to be both human and divine, we can conclude that the church itself is a kind of sacrament.

This, unfortunately, is also an outward sign to those who may visit. This type of outward sign indicates the congregation is in a complacent rut and not really interested in how it appears to others. The life of the congregation may be comfortable for those who are there, but by all signs, members aren't very interested in investing either resources or energy into making it more appealing for new people.

Vestries should conduct a "newcomers" tour of their building, to see it with new eyes. Start in the parking area and take the path a newcomer might. Notice the dead bushes next to the front door or the expensive oriental carpet in the gathering area, the accumulation of old memorials or the tattered boxes that have been under the back pews since 1957. What message is your building sending, both to newcomers and to your own members?

It is not necessary to have a huge budget in order to present an outward sign of care and involvement. I had the privilege of living in Honduras for several years. I visited many homes striking in their poverty. I have been to homes lacking basic things like running water, electricity, appliances, furniture, and even solid walls. Some of these homes almost breathe despair and neglect. They are dirty and disorganized and unpleasant. Other homes, some of the poorest, are kept clean and orderly and project an aura of hospitality. The people living in these homes obviously care about themselves and their families; they want to be part of the larger community and to offer a welcome to visitors. The difference is not money or lack thereof. The difference is effort and care.

A sacrament is not only a means but an end. Applying this concept to the buildings, I believe the outward appearance of the physical plant has a powerful effect on the spiritual life of a congregation. Worship in a building that is neglected and dirty is going to be compromised and depressed. Worship in a building that is a temple to the prosperity of the congregation will likewise be compromised. Our surroundings have a deep impact on us. What do you want your building and grounds to communicate to potential members, to your community, and to your congregation?

I suggest a few areas that you might consider:

First, do the facilities communicate basic healthiness? Imagine a church building that hasn't had a functional men's room in six months. The front door slams every time someone enters or leaves, the furnace barely functions, and the sound system makes everyone sound like they are speaking a foreign language. Is the congregation going to be credible in preaching hope of a better world? Since they are not even taking care of their own needs, will they be convincing when they offer help to others? What kind of prophetic witness can they have in addressing the problems of the world around them when they cannot find a way to stop the kitchen sink from dripping incessantly?

Second, does the church building itself welcome visitors? I cannot count the number of times I have visited a new church and literally not been able to figure out the entrance. Often it is unclear which door to enter, and doors that seem the obvious choices end up being locked. Issues like available parking, updated bulletin boards, and clear signage for restrooms and nursery space are outward and visible signs of inward health and vitality.

Third, does your building indicate that the congregation is living in this century or stuck in some other? Many congregations have inherited wonderful buildings, which can be a rich resource for worship and service. Some congregations have managed to keep these buildings alive and responsive to present concerns, while others have let the facilities become museums. This is evident even in what hangs on the walls. Take

> **Your physical property is an outward and visible sign of what you believe. Care for your building in such a way that it becomes a fit symbol for the amazing grace available in Christ.**

a look around. Memorials are fine, but at some point, if not properly managed, the entire church building becomes a monument to long-dead members. How depressing! Do you have any art rendered in the last ten years? The last twenty? Fifty? Is eating in the church dining room a visit to the 1940s? The 1970s? Has the sanctuary been repainted since the building was erected? Is the carpet so worn that new brides can easily follow the worn places to the front?

People live their lives in the present. The message many church buildings give is that in order to find God it is necessary to go back in time—and that this congregation cannot keep up with changes in the world.

There are other questions to ask, but the final one I will raise is important and often overlooked. "Is there anything winsome about the Christ you are presenting and proclaiming?" Are there refuges of beauty, of warmth, hospitality, or reverence in your building or grounds? Is there an attractive place where people can pray? Is there a bright and cheery place for folks to hold a meeting? Is there a bench under the trees where people can meditate? Are the vestments and church decorations in good shape and appropriate symbols of belief? Will the church artwork inspire or provoke thought? Is the rector's office a place of dignity that will convey trust and responsibility? Is there anything intriguing or attractive?

We present a Christ who offers healing, challenge, and hope—a new and passionate life. Although they will not think of this consciously, people will make a decision about whether or not to be involved in your church partly based on what they read from the building. They are searching for something in their lives. They will find a church that reflects the things they value. Is there anything about your building that says, "This is what we have become in Christ"?

Your physical property is an outward and visible sign of what you believe. Care for your building in such a way that it becomes a fit symbol for the amazing grace available in Christ.

FOR PERSONAL REFLECTION

Scripture says that our bodies are a temple for the Holy Spirit. These temples, of course, come in all shapes and sizes. Are you giving your body the care and respect it deserves?

FOR GROUP DISCUSSION

Take a field trip of your church from the point of view of a first-time visitor. What impression does the physical plant make? What does it say about your life together?

What influence does the building have on your worship together? Does it help to express who you are as a congregation? How might it improve?

CHAPTER FOUR

Filthy Lucre:
The Teaching of Jesus on Money

Do not store up for yourselves treasures on earth, where moth and rust consume and where thieves break in and steal; but store up for yourselves treasure in heaven, where neither moth nor rust consumes, and where thieves do not break in and steal. For where your treasure is, there your heart will be also. (Matthew 6:19-21)

I know what it is to have little, and I know what it is to have plenty. In any and all circumstances I have learned the secret of being well-fed and of going hungry, of having plenty and of being in need. I can do all things through him who strengthens me. (Philippians 4:12-13)

There is great gain in godliness combined with contentment; for we brought nothing into the world, so that we can take nothing out of it...For the love of money is a root of all kinds of evil, and in their eagerness to be rich some have wandered away from the faith and pierced themselves with many pains. (1 Timothy 6:6-7,10)

A surprisingly high percentage of the teachings of Jesus in the gospels has to do with the issue of money. He says very little about sexual behavior and nothing at all about church polity. But time after time Jesus comes back to the topic of money. He seems to consider money—and our relationship with it—a basic issue of faith. By contrast, we tend to view the use of our money as an advanced topic to be addressed only after we have our "feet on the ground financially" and have developed a mature faith. Unfortunately for our own comfort level, Jesus did not say "Where your heart is, there will your treasure be also." Instead, very radically, he said, "For where your treasure is, there your heart will be also" (Luke 12:34). Jesus indicates that shifting our wealth in order to invest in God's kingdom, by caring for those in need and building up the church, will result in a revival of faith. The way we use and allocate our resources gets to the core of our priorities, according to Jesus.

In the parable of the unjust steward in Luke (also called the parable of the dishonest manager), a manager is informed that he is being fired and he is ordered to get the accounts in order. He takes the opportunity to help the owner's clients falsify their accounts, reducing the amount they owe. When the owner discovers this, he actually commends the steward for his dishonesty and resourcefulness. The steward has used the owner's wealth to make friends for himself, hoping they will take care of him once he is out of a job. This parable is unsettling, but I think the interpretation is less complicated than we would like to believe. We are the stewards and have been given notice that our position will be terminated. (To put it bluntly, we are all going to die.) The unjust steward used the master's resources to buy friends for himself. Jesus marvels that we can figure out how to do that, but, faced with our obvious existential situation, we don't even try to put our money to use to make friends in heaven. He seems to commend such a thing! For Jesus, that is at least a beginning, and God will honor it.

Dealing with money is a basic responsibility of vestries. You are dealing not just with your own personal money, but with money donated by parishioners or funds left to you by previous generations. And you are dealing with this money as a group. We each bring to vestry business our own ideas about the role of money and its proper use. And for each one of us, these ideas will be very different. While many people today willingly discuss private details about relationships or family dynamics, discussion of personal finances is still considered a very personal area. This is because, for many people, money is the most important concern they have. This is true for both rich and poor, and for those in between.

Therein lies the challenge. We cannot be real disciples without addressing money issues. But at the same time, we are deeply uncomfortable with discussing money. The purpose of this chapter is not to address the practical questions about money that a vestry must confront. This will not answer how to put together a budget, or the proper balance between equities and bonds, or how to raise funds. This is a chance to take a step back and think about the attitudes we bring to issues involving money. As Christians acting together for Christ's church, how can we bring his teachings into our awareness in dealing with church finances?

What should be our model for how we talk about money? The gospels do not give us a sense that Jesus and his disciples traveled in luxury, but we know they had a treasurer and were supported by donations from others (John 13:29). We can also

> **We cannot be real disciples without addressing money issues.**

infer that some of those contributions were used to address the needs of those outside their group. For instance, when Judas left the Last Supper, the others assumed that he was, as usual, on his way to do an act of charity. Jesus did not accumulate money, but he paid taxes, bought food, and took care of the needs of his group of disciples.

In one sense, a modern congregation is simply a continuation of that group, with Jesus as the head of the church and parishioners as the disciples. With this premise as our guide, it's helpful to see what Jesus says about money.

Jesus seems to think that the money we have is not really ours. Over and over, he tells parables about workers taking care of someone else's vineyard (examples include Matthew 21:33-41 and Matthew 25:14-30). He reminds us that we are going to die. For this short while, we have resources put into our keeping, but ultimately we cannot lay claim to them. And we will be asked to give an account to God for the way we have used what we have been given.

Using Jesus' teachings on money as a compass, vestries need to act as stewards of the financial resources they have been given. They need to be responsible and act as those who will need to answer not only to the diocesan auditor but also to God. The church does not "own" money any more than we do as individuals. The way the church uses its money is a witness to its own members and its community of what it really believes. Keep in mind the parable of the talents: the servant who is condemned is the one who does not put what he has been given to work but literally buries it. The resources of a church are to be used, not buried.

Jesus indicates pretty clearly that possessing too much money is a spiritual impediment (Mark 10:17-25, Luke 12:13-21). How hard it is for the rich to enter into the kingdom of heaven! The rich young man turns away from Jesus because he has so much to lose. If we have money, the temptation is to rely on it and ultimately to lose touch with God, the giver of gifts. Jesus tells us in Luke 12 of the man who, very sensibly it seems, stores up money for the future so he can enjoy retirement but yet is considered a fool. The poor, hungry, and thirsty are the ones considered blessed in the beatitudes. The rich are in danger of being sent "empty away."

Jesus' words lead us to ask: how much money should a church have? This is a tough question. Considering that Jesus seems to be against accumulation, how should a church handle things like endowments?

In my opinion, a church should ideally address its operational needs through the pledges and gifts of members. I have seen too many churches spiritually emptied by long-term reliance on endowments. When everyone knows that a church has lots of money for programs and staff through large endowments and other funds, people choose either not to give or to give elsewhere. Go back to the words of Jesus about treasure and heart. If someone's treasure is not in the church, his or her heart will not be there, either. If members are giving, say, 20 percent of their income to a church, you can believe that they will be keeping pretty close track of the health of that parish.

Some churches have huge endowments and have become used to relying on them. Congregations should work toward operational independence from the endowment, so that those additional funds can be used to support outreach programs, a use fully in accord with what Jesus taught.

There are always exceptions. Some churches have inherited huge buildings from previous generations, and often these buildings are a financial drain. In that case, I think it is reasonable to have an endowment that covers the costs of that building. In other words, if you are left something for which you must be responsible, you also should have the resources to care for it.

Jesus considers the needs of the poor to be the responsibility of those who have more than enough (Matthew 25:31-46). The rich man in Jesus' graphic parable in chapter 16 of Luke is judged simply because he had too much and ignored the need on his doorstep. Jesus associates taking care of the needs of the poor with accumulating treasure in heaven, serving him, and loving God. He teaches us to pray for "our daily bread." We are not to pray that God will provide us as individuals with what we want but that God will provide us as a community with what we need. Sharing with one another is a logical extension of praying for our common needs: What I consider to be my possessions may be God's answer to the needs of the hungry.

Since Jesus is so insistent on caring for the needs of the poor, a vestry should also model that. There should be provision for outreach in the budget. This is money that should go for things other than the needs of the congregation. Many churches rely on extra fundraisers to meet the needs of others. While these extra activities are wonderful, not having a regular line item in the budget for outreach sends a strong message, teaching people that helping the poor is an extra, an afterthought, and not part of the structure of things.

In addition, I think it is healthy for a church to spend its resources each year rather than accumulate a large hedge against some rainy day. Luke 12 tells us that we are not to worry about financial things. God is a loving parent who knows we need basics and will provide the things we really need if we put the kingdom first. Preoccupation about financial worries puts us out of right relationship with God. Even when the supply looks short, and there are only five loaves and three fish for 5,000 hungry people, everyone still ends up with enough. We should pray for sufficiency and be thankful for that. There is no guarantee from God that we will have more than enough for this day's immediate need. If accumulating a surplus is the basis of our financial dealings, we are operating outside the realm of God's grace. In the US, we are steeped in a culture that touts accumulation of wealth. We should not forget how radical the approach of Jesus is.

This freedom from worry and compunction in financial matters opens us to new possibilities. Jesus values those who make sacrifices for the sake of the kingdom and who take risks for his sake. He points to the poor widow as the one who has made the most generous contribution because she has given from the little that she has (Luke 21:1-4). He commends those who leave fields and businesses and tax collectors' booths. When Zaccheus decides to make things right with others financially, Jesus says salvation has come to him (Luke 19:1-10).

Worry and preoccupation over the church budget tends to get a congregation out-of-whack spiritually. A large budget is not needed to ensure vitality. If spiritual vitality is present, if the church has a clear sense of mission, and if worship is celebrated with reverence and grace, the money tends to show up. Where there is a serious lack of funds, there is often a more fundamental problem.

Of course, there are exceptions to this premise. If a community is going through financial turmoil, with businesses shutting down and the neighborhood in decline, then the congregation will also usually experience financial stress. This is not faithlessness but comes from its identity with a suffering community. Still, worry and preoccupation are not what the congregation is called to demonstrate under these circumstances. There is still good news to be preached, healing to be offered, and community to be engendered. Vestry meetings need to grapple with financial matters, but they need to look at the things of the kingdom as well.

The vestry should share its vision with the rest of the parish. People do not generally get enthused about paying the sewage bill. That, of course, needs to be done, but the congregation does not exist to use water. They use water because they are gathering for other purposes. Communicate to the parish what the vestry is trying to accomplish. Remind them why they are gathering together. Give them a sense of where you are heading. Show some vision! If you do not have any vision or can't articulate one, then no one should give. There are better causes.

Vestry members are most effective when they model what they are asking the congregation to do. This means that you, as an individual, have an opportunity to grapple with the role of giving and money in your own life. I know from being in a parish for many years that churches do not function from the casual and infrequent gift. Churches live and thrive because some of their members have a discipline of giving proportionally. Usually 15 to 20 percent of members support over 80 percent of the budget. If another third of members gave in the same way, most churches would be in solid financial shape. You, as a vestry member, need to make a commitment to give in a disciplined and sacrificial way.

The issue of money is a central one for the life of a vestry. The vestry has the job of raising and spending funds for the church. This is an important spiritual responsibility as well as a practical management responsibility. The way a church uses money should reflect what Jesus taught about money. Think and pray about what Jesus teaches us, and try to make your financial decisions reflect that teaching.

FOR PERSONAL REFLECTION

How do I approach finances in my own life? Do I have a budget? Do I have savings? Do I have debt? What percentage of my income do I give to the church and toward other outside needs?

FOR GROUP DISCUSSION

What is our overall financial situation? Are we being good stewards of the resources we have?

In our stewardship programs, do we communicate to members our vision for ministry?

What statement does our financial approach make about our faith?

CHAPTER FIVE

The Church as the Body of Christ: Dealing with "Those" Vestry Members

God is faithful: by him you were called into the fellowship of his Son, Jesus Christ our Lord. Now I appeal to you, brothers and sisters, by the name of our Lord Jesus Christ, that all of you should be in agreement and that there should be no divisions among you, but that you be united in the same mind and the same purpose.
(1 Corinthians 1:9-10)

Now there are varieties of gifts, but the same Spirit; and there are varieties of services, but the same Lord; and there are varieties of activities, but it is the same God who activates all of them in everyone. To each is given the manifestation of the Spirit for the common good.
(1 Corinthians 12:4-7)

The wisdom from above is first pure, then peaceable, gentle, willing to yield, full of mercy and good fruits, without a trace of partiality or hypocrisy. (James 3:17)

One of the hardest parts of serving on a vestry is dealing with other vestry members. In the workplace, we have colleagues, but there is usually a hierarchy or system of accountability involved as well. The vestry is made up of volunteers, and you cannot really fire a vestry member, or put him or her on a performance improvement plan. In addition, sometimes vestry members are elected to grind a particular ax. And certainly the vestry is composed of different personalities, working styles, and vested interests. That can make it difficult to work together for a common cause.

Christianity is essentially a corporate religion. Those who worship at the same church are bound together. They are not simply a collection of folks who happen to be at the same place. They are not riding the elevator together, all with different destinations in mind. The relationships among members are not a byproduct of worshiping at the same place. The relationships are part of the essence of the church.

Jesus prayed that his disciples would be one so the world would know God sent him. Their unity as disciples and Jesus' credibility are joined together in his prayer (John 17:21). The love that they demonstrate for one another, and the unity they attain, are part of the gospel message they preach. His last commandment to his disciples was that they should love one another as he had loved them (John 13:34). The relationships we have as Christians with one another are part of the new life we have in Christ. They are not accidental or a burden to be borne. Because part of the richness of the Church is that it attracts all sorts of people, we are called into a fellowship that sometimes pushes us beyond our comfort levels.

From the beginning, this has been a challenge for the Church. Just dip into some of the epistles of Paul to understand that, in large part, these letters were written because members of the early church were not getting along. Then, as now, differing personalities, sensibilities, and theologies clashed with one another. Paul offered guidance then that is still relevant today.

In 1 Corinthians 12, Paul speaks of different members being like the various parts of a body. Of course they are not all alike! What would a body composed solely of ears look like? Or just eyes? Various members have different gifts, and each is to exercise his or her particular gift for the good of the Church. Once again, discernment comes into play. Vestry members are not all the same, not all ears or arms or legs. They must work together to help one another discern their unique gifts. The more vestry members free one another to exercise their particular gifts most fully, the happier everyone will be.

Let me give an example. Let's say that one vestry member is a retired engineer. He is concerned about lowering energy usage, both because of cost and because of care for creation. Because of his background as an engineer, he has done extensive studies on current electric and gas usage. He has, in a very thorough way, researched initial and long-term costs of making some changes, including replacing the light bulbs with energy-efficient LED ones and upgrading the furnace. He comes to the vestry meeting with a proposal to spend $12,000 now, which he believes will result in great savings in the future. He assumes other vestry members will want to approach this topic with the same care and exhaustive thoroughness. He has compiled charts, spreadsheets, technical specs, comparative bids, samples, and several articles on the impact of power-generating plants on global warming.

It is possible other members of the vestry may find this evening-long presentation less than riveting. One member runs her own successful business and is accustomed to deciding things on her own without debate. Another is passionate about the unrest in the Sudan and wants the vestry to fund a project for refugees. Another member loves the music program and wants to talk about its expansion. How are all these folks to meet in a way that will satisfy everyone?

It may sound obvious, but an important practice is to take time at the start of each new vestry term for people to get to know one other and learn something about the gifts each person brings. If vestry members understand the kind of care and the source of concern that motivates the engineer, they may want to assign him some of the nitty-gritty issues in the church and learn to trust his final recommendations. If members do not take the effort to get to know and appreciate one another, they are doomed to a series of misunderstandings and frustrations.

One method for identifying and sharing gifts is to take a personality inventory (MMPI, StrengthsFinder, and Enneagram are some popular programs). These tools can help members understand one another, their leadership styles, and their motivations. It can help identify who loves process, who needs quick resolution, who needs to be encouraged to speak, and who might need to be gently muzzled. The important thing is that members acknowledge and appreciate one another so that the time on vestry can be one of growing closer, not something that leads to resentment and division.

I spent six years in ministry in Honduras and learned a lot from my coworkers there. One of the things that impressed me most in Honduras is the emphasis on relationship over achievement. Another is the desire to make sure that we are all grounded together in our faith.

Many vestry meetings open with prayer and meditation. My experience is that this is often a token time to remind members that they are not meeting as the board of the country club but as a church. In Honduras, I found that things functioned differently. I began one of my first meetings with a bit of scripture and a few remarks. Then I asked if any of the other participants had anything to add. Remarkably, they jumped in with such enthusiasm that we did not get to the business part of the meeting for more than an hour. We talked about the scripture, what it meant to us, and how we thought it applied to our shared ministry. Then, having opened ourselves, we prayed for each other.

Interestingly, when we turned to the business, we did so in a united way and accomplished a remarkable amount. More importantly, long after that particular meeting was done, the relationships and cooperation among the staff continued to grow and flourish.

> Just as the doctrine of the Incarnation teaches us that the church is both human and divine, so, in vestries, two factors need to be held in tension: the work and the relationships.

Just as the doctrine of the Incarnation teaches us that the church is both human and divine, so, in vestries, two factors need to be held in tension: the work and the relationships. What the vestry accomplishes is important. The relationships between members are equally important. Unless both are considered, the vestry will not be what it is called to be. A vestry in which a few highly effective people push through a good agenda but at the expense of input from other members is not functioning as it should. A vestry that is primarily a support group for its members is also inappropriate. The ideal we strive for is a healthy balance of accomplishments and relationships, but we are all still on our own pilgrimage toward holiness, and no vestry I know of has reached this balance yet.

Many vestries have one or two difficult people who seem to obstruct business, who are always feeling offended, or who are always offending others, or who will stay silent during the meeting and then complain about the decisions the vestry has just made. What does it mean to try to include and love these people?

This is the time for those in leadership to assert themselves. Sometimes the wardens and/or clergy need to have a private meeting with an individual and confront the issue(s). This may be an opportunity for that person to learn something about him or herself. The vestry should not be held hostage to any one individual, nor should a congregation be subjected to strife and division that comes from a member subverting the work of the vestry.

Some of this kind of strife can be prevented with responsible screening before elections. A nominating committee can make recommendations about who should be running for vestry. That committee should contact their priest before contacting the persons involved. He or she may know good reasons why vestry service at that particular time is not a good thing. This is not discrimination. It is a way of discerning within the Body of Christ the roles each member should play.

On the subject of difficult people, it is also important for you to consider the possibility that you are that person for others. If you continually come home from vestry meetings frustrated that the rest of the group isn't listening to you, or you believe they're headed in the wrong direction, being blind and irresponsible, it is quite possible that you are fulfilling a prophetic ministry in that congregation. It is, however, even more possible that you are coming across as arrogant and obstructionist, or as irrelevant and ineffective. In either case, this is a chance for growth for you as a person. Remember, all conversions begin with a recognition that there is something that needs to be changed. Our faith gives us the assurance that the discomfort of confronting these problems within ourselves is worth it because God graciously helps us grow in grace.

The first group of twelve disciples traveled with Jesus, experiencing with him the ups and downs of his ministry and learning from him. At the end of their time with him, during the Last Supper, Jesus did not give them an agenda for future accomplishments but rather the directive to love one another as he had loved them. Only after that did he charge them to go into the world. As vestry members, learning to care, appreciate, and work for the good of the other members is your first charge. How might your meetings change if each member came with that clear conviction?

FOR PERSONAL REFLECTION

What are your own personal quirks? What kinds of things set you off? What positive traits do you bring to a group process?

FOR GROUP DISCUSSION

How much do we know about each other?

What gifts do we recognize in the members of this vestry?

Do we leave meetings feeling energized or drained? Why?

CHAPTER SIX

Treasure in Clay Pots: Care of Clergy

Blessed be the God and Father of our Lord Jesus Christ, the Father of mercies and the God of all consolation, who consoles us in all our affliction, so that we may be able to console those who are in any affliction with the consolation with which we ourselves are consoled by God. For just as the sufferings of Christ are abundant for us, so also our consolation is abundant through Christ. (2 Corinthians 1:3-5)

In the presence of God and of Christ Jesus, who is to judge the living and the dead, and in view of his appearing and his kingdom, I solemnly urge you: proclaim the message; be persistent whether the time is favorable or unfavorable; convince, rebuke and encourage, with the utmost patience in teaching. (2 Timothy 4:1-2)

For we do not proclaim ourselves; we proclaim Jesus Christ as Lord and ourselves as your slaves for Jesus' sake. For it is the God who said, "Let light shine out of darkness," who has shone in our hearts to give the light of the knowledge of the glory of God in the face of Jesus Christ. But we have this treasure in clay jars, so that it may be made clear that this extraordinary power belongs to God and does not come from us. (2 Corinthians 4:5-7)

One of the main responsibilities of a vestry is working with the rector, vicar, or other clergy person assigned to the parish. In the absence of a rector, it is the vestry's responsibility to find and call a new one and lead the congregation during the interim and transition. And, of course, the vestry ends up being the body that determines the rector's pay.

It's important to understand ordination and what it means to serve the church in that capacity. The priest or deacon is often dealt with as if he/she is an employee meant to fulfill the will of the vestry, or, on the other extreme, as if he/she is in a privileged relationship with the Creator and should always be considered right. Neither of these opinions is helpful.

My daughter once saw a book advertised that made the bold claim that clergy were human. Her response was "Duh!" She had seen me in all-too-human terms. This is not really a point that should need to be made, but in the interest of caution, I will make it anyway. Clergy are human. As such, we, like all people, are sinful and in need of redemption and reform of life. We are capable of doing stupid and sinful things and of being wrong even about important things like the nature of God. We have periods of self-pity and are working through various issues. We get along with some people better than others, we are tempted by money, physical attraction, and in many other ways, and we have strengths and weaknesses. We have bad habits and our own particular idiosyncrasies. For some reason, known only to God, God has chosen to work through human beings. I doubt I would have set things up that way, but I am not in charge, and God must have a good reason. But it means that in choosing church leadership, human beings are what we have to pick from.

One crucial theological point to remember: your clergy person is in the process of redemption just as you are. It would add sense and clarity to the situation if he or she were, so to speak, more advanced on that path than the rest of the congregation. But I do not believe there is such a simple scale, and I have become convinced that, even if there were, plenty of people in the congregation would be further along the path than the priest. It is not the job of the priest to be the most spiritual person in the parish. It is not even desirable. That is not the point at all.

The priest is meant to be the person who holds the gospel before the congregation, and who also, through prayer and pastoral care, holds the congregation before God. The congregation, in turn, is meant to hold that same gospel before the world and to hold the world before God. We are all helped in that mission by the presence of God's Spirit in our lives. Once again we have one of those polarities: we are all sinners in need of grace, and we are all saints with a gospel to proclaim and a role to play in God's saving work.

> **My daughter once saw a book advertised that made the bold claim that clergy were human. Her response was "Duh!"**

Sometimes it is easy to lose track of this work of holding the people before God and God before the people. Being a parish priest is one of the few remaining general practitioner jobs. The priest is expected to write and deliver interesting and probing sermons. He or she is also expected to be a good organizer and leader of liturgy. In addition, the priest should be a comforting and inspiring presence to those who are ill or going through loss. The priest is to be adept at one-on-one counseling on every topic, from marriage problems to troubled teenagers to moral dilemmas at work to dealing with an elderly parent.

Meanwhile, there are the ongoing issues of organizing congregational life, making sure the building and finances are in good order, and tending to any disputes. Of course, the clergy person also is expected to be involved in community and diocesan duties, without sacrificing any of the time he or she needs to prepare to teach the adult forum. It is really good for the young people of the parish to have time with the rector, and ditto for the children, to whom he or she is expected to give a short but lucid sermon while the rest of the congregation watches. If there is a staff, the rector is also in charge of hiring and directing such staff. All this is done while cultivating a faithful prayer life and keeping up on current reading and seminars so that sermons do not get stale.

No one person can be good at all these things. As in the case of determining the gifts of vestry members, it is worthwhile for the vestry to work with the priest to determine the best way to maximize his or her gifts and supplement the weaknesses. Some priests are excellent at being up front: they preach wonderful sermons and have a wonderful presence in leading liturgy. But that same person may be horrible at organizing events or enlisting volunteers or giving direction to the staff. Some parishes hire an administrator who can assist with these duties. Other priests may excel at organization, be warm and incisive counselors, and have a real gift at hospital ministry but be lackluster in the pulpit. A vestry might consider bringing in a guest preacher once a month to supplement the ministry of preaching.

The priest is not meant to be a one-person ministry team. He or she functions in community, and the vestry should seek ways to offer support and encouragement so that the ministry the priest offers can be more effective.

Often churches fail to support their clergy in productive ways. Some congregations focus solely on the weaknesses of the priest. Besides creating a negative and discouraging atmosphere, this attitude tends to become a self-perpetuating pattern. Clergy talk among themselves. A critical, judgmental church will develop a reputation. When competent clergy hear about this reputation, they will choose not to come to such a place. So, even if the present "incompetent" rector leaves, the list of those who desire to replace him or her is not going to be the "A" list. And so the cycle continues.

Another pattern is simply to passively endure the weaknesses of a particular clergy person. That means that during a priest's tenure, some things will prosper, and others will go into a kind of dormancy. I think this is a failure by the vestry to take their share of responsibility for supporting the ministries of the church. Much better to have the wardens, or some other group appointed by the vestry with the agreement of the rector, actively seek ways to maximize the gifts of the priest and to augment those areas in which he or she may be weak.

The church is the community where people gather to grapple with the place of God in their lives, and the priest is a person whose teachings and example bear heavily on members' understanding of God. In a sense, the stakes are high. Some members of the church will inevitably have very strong feelings about the teaching or the life of the priest.

Sometimes priests commit actions so serious that the vestry must address them. These problems include (but are not limited to): financial mismanagement, having an affair, missing services or appointments because of addictions, or being abusive to staff members. Dioceses have systems in place to address these problems. The bishop is the chief pastor of the diocese, and he or she should be informed and consulted if any such serious issues arise.

Serious inappropriate actions need a serious response. At the same time, the vestry should take care to discern the situation. Sometimes a faction of the congregation may fall into grumbling about their priest, which then travels down a slippery slope to gossip and suspicion. If there is a clear violation of ethics or pastoral responsibility, then this should be dealt with openly and in accordance with the procedures specified by the diocese. If not, rumors and undercutting need to be stopped.

Who will want to join a church divided into factions? Who will want to become part of a community that judges one of its members so harshly? Who will feel safe if the foibles of another, who gives so much, are regarded with scorn and rejection? I believe there is a spiritual and emotional connection between priest and people that makes this a destructive process.

Another perspective to consider is the emotional toll of serving as a priest. The priest carries all sorts of secrets that have to do with the saddest and most difficult parts of the lives of the members of the congregation. The priest spends a lot of time in situations of crisis and sadness, visiting the dying and then conducting the funeral liturgy. The priest visits with the homebound or those in nursing homes. He or she offers marriage counseling or help with addictions. The priest listens to confession, either formal or informal.

What are priests to do with all of this sadness and fear and sin? One temptation is to become callous, cynical, or distant. At the same time, priests are called to love and support the members of the congregation. To be a priest, to hold the people before God, means embracing their suffering and sins also. Priests carry the most vulnerable and frail aspects of the congregation in their hearts and minds.

When a congregation turns on its priest, it attacks the one who cares for its own heart. How is a priest to offer spiritual guidance or encouragement in the face of hostility and resentment? The Old Testament includes provision for a "scapegoat," an animal loaded with the sins of the people and then driven away into the wilderness (Leviticus 16:20-22). A priest is not meant to be such a scapegoat. Yet many priests have experienced crises in their ministries and were treated like the scapegoat. In some cases, the individuals behind parish discord were those whose sins and weaknesses had been revealed to the priest. Since confidentiality is a basic commitment of clergy, the priest is at a kind of disadvantage. He or she cannot really fight back without violating the sanctity of his or her own ministry. It will not do to say, "He wants me out of here because I know about his affair." When the relationship between clergy and people becomes mired in suspicion, mistrust, and hurt, the parish loses much of its vitality. Mutual ministry requires vulnerability, and it is hard to remain vulnerable while under attack.

In some parishes, a regular "mutual review" takes place between the priest and congregational leaders. This formal process helps make sure that both priest and congregation are talking about how to work toward health for the congregation. It is

> Clergy, like the rest of us, are a mix between saint and sinner.

helpful for the priest to know what the congregation wants from him or her, and what aspects of his or her ministry are most appreciated. It is helpful for the wardens or other representatives of the congregation to hear what the priest desires from them—as well as for the priest to offer thanksgiving for their past (and hopefully, continuing) support. This kind of ongoing and constructive conversation has a tendency to spread throughout the parish, so that even groups that have been arguing among themselves for decades begin to feel a bit out of place and may change their way of being.

Clergy, like the rest of us, are a mix between saint and sinner. They are not omnipotent or omniscient, infallible or motivated solely by steadfast love and faithfulness. A congregation that helps the ministry of the clergy thrive usually finds its own ministry flourishes as well. If one member of the body is healthy, that health spreads to the other members.

FOR PERSONAL REFLECTION

What do you look for in your clergy? What do others look for in you?

Has your life been enriched in any way by clergy? How do you minister to others in the church?

FOR GROUP DISCUSSION

Do we have a mutual ministry evaluation process? How effective is it? How could we improve the process?

What things could we do as a vestry to support our clergy?

CHAPTER SEVEN

Go Into All the World: Parish Mission

Then the disciples rejoiced when they saw the Lord. Jesus said to them again, "Peace be with you. As the Father has sent me, so I send you." (John 20:20b-21)

Jesus came and said to them, "All authority in heaven and on earth has been given to me. Go therefore and make disciples of all nations, baptizing them in the name of the Father and of the Son and of the Holy Spirit, and teaching them to obey everything that I have commanded you. And remember, I am with you always, to the end of the age." (Matthew 28:18-20)

Then the king will say to those at his right hand, "Come, you that are blessed by my Father, inherit the kingdom prepared for you from the foundation of the world; for I was hungry and you gave me food, I was thirsty and you gave me something to drink, I was a stranger and you welcomed me, I was naked and you gave me clothing. I was sick and you took care of me, I was in prison and you visited me." (Matthew 25:34-36)

*Will you proclaim by word and example the Good News of God in Christ? Will you seek and serve Christ in all persons, loving your neighbor as yourself? Will you strive for justice and peace among all people, and respect the dignity of every human being? I will, with God's help. (*The Book of Common Prayer, *The Baptismal Covenant)*

In some ways, a parish functions as a family. A family is meant to be a structure that supports and nurtures its members so that they can grow into healthy persons and take their role in the world. Much of the pastoral ministry in a congregation is geared toward this kind of model. And from this perspective, it makes little sense to talk about a parish needing a "mission," just as you would not urge a family to have a specific mission.

> **A focus on survival rather than mission is a path to shrinking membership and fiscal disaster.**

The church, however, is more than a familial support group. God has entrusted the church with a mission. We are to carry on the ministry of Christ through proclamation and example. As Archbishop William Temple said more than a century ago, the church exists for those who are not our members. Jesus has sent us into the world to share the gospel and given us a responsibility to care for the poor and the homeless, the stranger and the helpless. If a parish focuses all of its energy on its members, then the church is not living into the commission given by Christ to go and make disciples. The congregation becomes self-focused and complacent, and ultimately, irrelevant. Congregations are not to be reclusive, exclusive guardians of the gospel but places committed to going into the world in the power of the Holy Spirit.

The shape of this mission will vary by congregation, and each must discern its own ministry in a particular time and place. For a large parish with generous resources of both finances and leadership, it may seem easier to rise to this sense of mission (although there are challenges inherent in size, scope, and commitment for large churches too). But many Episcopal congregations struggle with balancing a budget built on building and personnel costs. During times of financial difficulty, outreach is often the first area cut from the budget. When outreach is considered a luxury, not a necessity, in a church's budget, we lose sight of the gospel. And if that's not enough to shift priorities, then consider this: in most situations, a focus on survival rather than mission is a path to shrinking membership and fiscal disaster. The goal of being gathered into a parish community is not simply to keep the doors open a few years longer. My experience is that when congregations focus on themselves, they begin to fall apart. In God's economy, we prosper when we focus on the needs of others. This is the kind of attitude God seems to bless and encourage. It even makes sense psychologically. Which church would you rather join: one in which the members regard you as "fresh blood" who may keep their congregation alive a bit longer, or a place in which the members are eagerly working together on an exciting mission to others?

Understanding that mission is vital is the first step. The next step is determining the mission for a particular parish. The process varies from parish to parish. Canonically, establishing the mission is not expressly the job of the vestry. Sometimes the rector articulates a strong sense of mission that is accepted by the parish. Sometimes the parish has a sense of its own mission and calls a rector to help live that out. Other times a committee of the vestry works with the rector and church leaders to help discern the mission or an outside consultant helps a parish understand its mission more clearly.

In whatever scenario, vestry support of the mission is crucial. No church has unlimited resources, in money or leadership, so these resources need to be allocated carefully and thoughtfully. The vestry must talk about and understand the mission of the parish in order to make appropriate decisions about budget and priorities. This may mean switching funds from an area that was once vibrant but is no longer central to the mission. This won't be easy, but a vestry focused on a unifying mission will have the courage to make tough decisions.

Parish missions are as varied as congregations and communities. Every parish has specific geographical and historical space, parishioners with certain gifts and passions, and particular needs and opportunities in the community. The mission of a church grows out of prayer, engagement, and discernment, taking all these factors into account.

I once served in a small, inner-city mission. We were on the border between a very poor neighborhood that was mostly African American and a section of the city that was being gentrified by young white professionals. We were an interracial parish and desired very much to continue to be so. We believed that part of our mission was to be a witness of love, creativity, and energy from different groups coming together. But we were faced with the question of how to reach out to two different populations at the same time. Where were the points of intersection?

We talked about developing a jazz worship service. Jazz is, after all, the product of two very different musical cultures, black and white, coming together. Many of the people in the black community were jazz aficionados, and we found that many of our white professionals were also jazz fans. The only trouble was that we did not have the resources to pull together such a service. So we prayed about that and other possibilities.

As if in answer to our prayers, one day the doorbell of my office rang, and two young men asked about the abandoned buildings across the street. I invited them in and showed them around the church. They had just moved from New York and were jazz musicians. They offered to help us start a jazz service. We already had creative people skilled in dance, poetry reading, and drama who joined the effort. We began a regular jazz service several afternoons each month. Within a year, the jazz service attracted a full house. I am happy to say that it is still going twenty years later.

This mission would not work for every congregation. But it was the right fit for that inner-city church, based on the situation and needs at that particular time. A large, downtown church is bound to have a different kind of mission than a smaller church in a rural community. A church with a large endowment will have a different sort of mission than one that struggles to pay the heating bill. The nature of the neighborhood and of the congregation, the experience and gifts of the priest and the members, the physical plant, the style of worship, and many other factors all enter into finding the right focus or mission for a particular parish.

Mission also changes over time, and the vestry can provide leadership and resources for the church to fulfill what God is calling it to do at any point in history. The vestry has the power to move financial resources to particular areas of mission. It has the authority to authorize the rector to hire staff people to fulfill mission objectives, and the vestry has a say in making the building and grounds available for that mission. If the vestry members do not have a sense of the overall mission of the church, none of these things will happen.

FOR PERSONAL REFLECTION

What are some of the gifts you personally have to offer? What are some qualities or talents that others have mentioned about you with appreciation?

FOR GROUP DISCUSSION

Do we as a vestry have a good sense of the character and needs of the community around us? How do those needs fit within our mission as a church?

Do we encourage the members of our congregation to use their talents and gifts in ministry to others?

What do we currently do as outreach?

CHAPTER EIGHT

Redemption and Sanctification: Stability and Change

Jesus Christ is the same yesterday and today and forever. (Hebrews 13:8)

But many who are first will be last, and the last will be first. (Matthew 19:30)

So let us not grow weary in doing what is right, for we will reap at the harvest-time, if we do not give up. (Galatians 6:9)

*Thereby the whole congregation was put in mind of the message of pardon and absolution set forth in the Gospel of our Savior, and of the need which all Christians continually have to renew their repentance and faith. (*The Book of Common Prayer, *Ash Wednesday)*

A common conflict in parish life is between those who are heavily invested in continuing beloved traditions and practices and those who are eager to change and innovate. In my experience a parish is more likely to be weighted toward tradition than change. Many clergy are accustomed to hearing about how wonderful things were under blessed Father Venerable, who has been retired for decades. Members of a parish are there because the life of that congregation has sustained and enriched them. It is understandable that they have a strong desire to conserve what has been meaningful. It is also clear that the world is rapidly changing—and that the church must change in order to respond to the needs of that world. Stability and change are both necessary for a healthy congregation.

Stability and change might seem like mutually exclusive qualities, but both are necessary for life and growth and need to be held in balance. In my experience, many churches like to get into a groove, to find a pattern or approach that seems to work, and then to stay with that as long as possible. This is stability. Many people enjoy knowing what to expect when they go to worship or sign up for a committee. And there's value in reliability and predictability. But stability in itself, without the balancing pull of change, easily deteriorates into rigidity, boredom, and paralysis.

> **Stability and change are both necessary for a healthy congregation.**

Change can bring freshness and new life. The elements of change are the ones that catch our attention most often; we are more likely to notice a break in our routine than we are to notice the everyday predictable events. But if change is not held in tension with stability, it degenerates into chaos and disorder. A church that changes its service times every week, has a random series of visiting preachers, or does outreach based on the whims of members is a hard church to join.

Our liturgy reflects this balance. In The Episcopal Church, each week the structure of the liturgy is essentially the same, following *The Book of Common Prayer*. But the basic structure is fleshed out with elements of change: new readings, a variety of hymns, and hopefully a different sermon. Human beings seem to like spontaneity and change—but with some limits.

This balance between stability and change is reflected in the gospel. Yes, Jesus is the same yesterday, today, and forever, and the faith we proclaim is based on that proclaimed by the apostles almost two thousand years ago. But the world has changed, and the situations we face as Christians have changed. And how we live out our faith also must change. If we toss the fundamental premises of the gospel up in the air, then we no longer have a church. At the same time, if we cling only to old understandings and ways of doing things, then we have a church unable to communicate with the world.

Repentance, transformation, and resurrection are words with great importance for Christians. The call of Jesus to us is not one that simply adds perks to our already happy state. Jesus calls us to move from death to life, slavery to freedom, darkness to light. In God's coming kingdom, the first will be last, and the least will be the greatest. To follow the invitation of Jesus is to give up old patterns and be willing to be made new by the Spirit. It involves radical change.

A certain amount of change is required by the most basic call of Christ: "The time is fulfilled, and the kingdom of God has come near; repent, and believe the good news!" (Mark 1:15b). In Greek, the word for repent literally means to have a new mind. It means to turn around. It means to change one's thoughts and behavior. This is the good news we receive and grapple with.

The Puritans believed this radical need for change meant there was nothing good in humanity. But in the Anglican tradition, we view this need for change in light of Jesus' resurrection. We believe the image of God is in every human being. As Anglicans, we acknowledge the need for change, but we also profess that God pronounced creation as good, and therefore we do not need to give up our humanity in order to follow Jesus. In fact, Jesus seems to see holiness in the everyday parts of life. Each meal is a gift of God's generosity. A cup of cold water holds a blessing. Those who persevere on the path are the ones who eventually reach their destination. There's the wrenching change of repentance, but we also value steady growth, stability, and faithfulness as part of our spiritual discipline. We need both change and stability.

A strand of Christianity interprets the call for repentance as a one-time thing. Once you become a Christian, then you are forever facing a new direction and no longer need to repent. (That sort of makes things easy! Yes, you needed to change, but you made the decision in the past and now everyone else needs to change to be more like you.) Mainstream Christian tradition, including Anglicanism, holds that repentance is a lifelong process that leads us to the likeness of Christ. In other words, the Christian life is a series of repentances, each bringing us closer to Christ. This process is known as sanctification.

This is the case for congregations as well as for individuals. Congregations are meant to be actively walking the road of transformation into the image of Christ. No congregation is an already perfect image of Christ. We are all engaged together in this process of sanctification through repentance and growth.

While few argue with this view from a theological position, the application is tricky. It is one thing to make a theological statement or a general confession. It is quite another to come to embrace change. Often people are invested in the ways things are (or used to be), and they probably are content to leave them alone. No matter what we may think in general about being fallen and sinful human beings, not many of us like to have the specifics of our fallen state brought to our attention. Further, I think few, if any, congregations or church groups are purposefully closed and rigid, bound to outdated practices and attitudes that are no longer productive. And yet, many churches eventually fall into that category. Somewhere along the line, they lose their ability to follow the path of constructive repentance.

The seminal story of the Old Testament is the journey the Israelites take from slavery toward freedom. Having been released and delivered from Pharaoh, they still have a journey to make, both geographically and spiritually, before they are ready for the Promised Land. It turns out that the spiritual journey takes a lot more time than the geographical one. This exodus is a powerful metaphor for our own journey as individuals and congregations. God has released us from sin and from the power of death, but we are in need of transformation before we get to the kingdom. Through the Israelites' journey, transformation involved elements of radical change (crossing of the Red Sea, receiving the Ten Commandments) and decades of stability (daily manna, the pillar of cloud and fire), during which the people learned of God's steadfast love and faithfulness. Both stability and change were part of their growth and transformation.

So we see that sanctification is a process that takes place in two main ways: change and consolidation. Consider a parallel to a child's physical development. Crawling is a fine mode of transportation for a while, but then the child attempts to walk. This is a period of conflict and falling and running into obstacles, but eventually the child masters this new way of getting around. After walking is mastered, it is time to learn to run, ride a bike, or drive. Each stage has a period of uncertainty and risk and sometimes failure, but eventually, through time and practice, the new skill is consolidated and becomes the norm.

> **A healthy vestry has both reformers and traditionalists represented—and they respect each other and value what they bring to the table.**

In his letter to the Philippians, Paul encourages Christians by saying that the work God has begun in them is one God will bring to completion. It is advice we do well to remember today. Every congregation is on the road toward being made complete in Christ. There will be times on that journey in which we will need to change course, find a new skill, reevaluate our way of doing things, give up a sinful pattern, come to terms with a limitation, take on a new responsibility, or adjust our vision. Other times, we are meant to patiently walk through each day, being faithful to the commitments and understanding that we have already been given.

A vestry is charged with balancing these two elements. Part of the work of the vestry is to provide structure and continuity. Bills need to be paid, staff need to be hired, the building needs to be cared for, etc. The other part of the work of the vestry is to help lead the congregation through healthy change. After all, we are not yet in the promised land.

Within a vestry, different folks will speak out on behalf of these two perspectives. A healthy church is one that can listen to a challenge to change without becoming threatened or reactionary. It is also a church that can faithfully follow a path that has been decided upon through careful discernment. Most congregations will experience some degree of stability and change at the same time. The program for pastoral care may be on a clear path, while the music program needs to go through radical change. The outreach program may be considering new initiatives, while the buildings and grounds folks push for care of the present facility.

Instead of vilifying people who push for change or criticizing those who advocate for consistency with the past, we should see that both viewpoints have value. It may help a vestry to acknowledge that conflict about how and whether to change is inevitable. It cannot be avoided. It should not be avoided. But it does not need to be destructive conflict. Discussions may touch on issues that expose areas of sensitivity or challenge long-accepted practices and beliefs. That is okay. Attempting to resolve conflict by personal attacks, belittling and dismissing the arguments of others, and in general trying to do away with opposition, is not acceptable.

Paul says that we are more than conquerors through Christ (Romans 8:37). Conquerors win, but they win at a cost. They still have enemies, albeit ones who have, for the present, become powerless. If we are able to listen to one another and resolve our differences with respect, then we are better off than those who conquer. We have formed a new and creative union.

A healthy vestry has both reformers and traditionalists represented—and they respect each other and value what they bring to the table. God does not call us to change for change's sake, with an unquestioned embrace of every new trend. God also does not call us to remain as we were but to continue our common pilgrimage toward the kingdom. Growth in Christ means change, but it also means continuity. What God taught us in the past is not out of sync with what God will ask of us in the future.

A vestry leads a congregation, through its decisions about staff, budget, and policies, toward a fuller life in Christ. If vestry members can honor both those who are agents of change and those who are agents of stability, the church will move forward in the right direction, living into God's call to love and serve.

FOR PERSONAL REFLECTION

Have there been times in your life when it was crucial to persevere in spite of difficulties or doubts?

Have there been times in your life in which it was important to make major changes?

How did you know the difference?

FOR GROUP DISCUSSION

What activities, attitudes, and traditions are precious to us and need to be nurtured and continued?

Are there norms, activities, or customs that could be changed for the better?

About the author

Richard Kunz is rector of Grace/La Gracia Episcopal Church in White Plains, New York, where he has served since 2010. Prior to that, he was an appointed missioner of The Episcopal Church serving in Honduras for six years as executive director of El Hogar Projects, an outreach ministry working with children and young people who come from severe poverty. He also has served in Princeton, New Jersey, and Pittsburgh, Pennsylvania.

A portion of the proceeds of this book have been donated to El Hogar Projects. Learn more about this important ministry at www.elhogar.org.

About Forward Movement

Forward Movement is committed to inspiring disciples and empowering evangelists. While we produce great resources like this book, Forward Movement is not a publishing company. We are a ministry.

Our mission is to support you in your spiritual journey, to make stronger disciples and followers of Jesus Christ. Publishing books, daily reflections, studies for small groups, and online resources is an important way that we live out this ministry. More than a half million people read our daily devotions through *Forward Day by Day*, which is also available in Spanish (*Adelante Día a Día*) and Braille, online, as a podcast, and as an app for your smartphones or tablets. It is mailed to more than fifty countries, and we donate nearly 30,000 copies each quarter to prisons, hospitals, and nursing homes. We actively seek partners across the Church and look for ways to provide tools that inspire and challenge.

A ministry of The Episcopal Church for more than seventy-five years, Forward Movement is a nonprofit organization completely funded by sales of resources and gifts from generous donors. To learn more about Forward Movement and our resources, please visit us at www.forwardmovement.org or www.AdelanteEnElCamino.org.

We are delighted to be doing this work and invite your prayers and support.